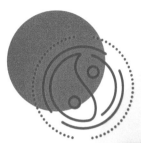

AILEEN LOZADA KIM

TRADITIONAL CHINESE MEDICINE

made easy!

A BEGINNER'S GUIDE TO

ACUPUNCTURE & HERBAL MEDICINE

THIS IS AN AILEEN LOZADA KIM
CHILDREN'S BOOK

Published in 2020 by
Aileen Lozada Kim

Text, design and illustration
© Aileen Lozada Kim 2020

ISBN: 978-1-7350575-0-7

A catalogue record for this book is available
from the British Library.

Author: Aileen Lozada Kim
Design: Clare Baggaley
         www.clarebaggaley.graphics
Editor: Lisa Edwards

The publishers would like to thank the
following sources for their kind permission
to reproduce the pictures in this book.

SHUTTERSTOCK.COM cover pictures
(except post-it note), pages 1, 2-3, 4-5
(except bruising art), 6-7 (except small yin
yang symbol), 8, 10, 12 (top icon), 14-15
(except ear art and acupressure), 16-17
(except bruising art), 18-19 (main image),
20-21 (teas and doctor), 24-25 (icons),
26-27 (cupping and 5 elements), 28-29
(except tongue), 30-31 and the black line art
icons throughout. FREEPIK.COM pages 7
(small yin yang icon), 14 (acupressure) 18
(small vegetables), 20-23 and on cover (post-it
notes), 22-23 (except artworks), 24-25 (doctor
and clipboards), 26 (doctors and yin yang
symbol). AILEEN LOZADA KIM artworks on
pages 4 (bruising), 9, 10-11, 12-13, 15 (ear), 16
(bruising), 20-25 (tongues and pulses), 27 (poop), 28
(tongue), all © Aileen Lozada Kim.

Every effort has been made to acknowledge correctly
and contact the source and/or copyright holder of
each image. We apologize for any unintentional errors
or omissions, which will be corrected on future
editions of this book.

This book is intended for anyone
who is interested in learning more about the
human body or who is curious about natural
medicine – maybe even someone who aspires to
become a doctor of natural medicine one day. Traditional
Chinese Medicine is a form of natural medicine but this book
should not be considered a medical textbook and should not
be used to diagnose or treat any health conditions. The
information provided in this book provides a basic insight and
understanding into Traditional Chinese Medicine only and
does not replace medical advice from physicians.
*For a diagnosis and/or treatment of any type,
consult your physician*.

CONTENTS

WHAT IS TRADITIONAL CHINESE MEDICINE?

Traditional Chinese Medicine (TCM) is a form of **natural medicine** that has been practiced for over 2,000 years and is still being practiced today.

In English: Chinese medicine
In Chinese: 中医 (Zhōng Yī)
Say: *Jong Ee*

TCM is mainly known for acupuncture and herbal medicine. **Acupuncture** is a treatment method that uses thin needles to stimulate points on the body. **Herbal medicine** is the use of herbs to make medicinal recipes. But TCM also includes other forms of treatments such as **Tuina** massage, a type of medical treatment that uses massage to stimulate points on the body; **cupping** therapy – the use of suction cups to stimulate points on the body to help the flow of blood and energy; **food therapy**, which is the use of healthy food to balance the body and stay healthy, and a type of exercise called **Qigong**. Qigong is an exercise that combines breathing, movements and meditation in order to improve one's health.

You can find descriptions of the key words in bold in the glossary on page 30

WHAT IS THE DIFFERENCE BETWEEN WESTERN MEDICINE AND TRADITIONAL CHINESE MEDICINE?

Western medicine uses scientific evidence to identify a problem and then uses surgery or drugs as a treatment. While this method can be good for some people, it isn't always the best option for everyone. Drugs may have harmful side effects, which can make them dangerous. On the other hand, Traditional Chinese Medicine uses several theories, such as the **Yin Yang Theory**, the **Qi Theory**, and the **Five Elements Theory** to identify a problem. It then uses acupuncture and herbal recipes as a treatment, which are milder methods that target the whole body (body, mind, and spirit).

Unlike Western medicine, TCM treatments are more personalized because everyone's body is different and they may experience different symptoms, even if they have the same illness. Therefore, TCM focuses on identifying a patient's body condition to correctly personalize a treatment. Both Western medicine and natural medicine are very useful – and for this reason, it is best that each person asks a well-informed doctor whether TCM is a good treatment option for their specific health problem.

WHAT IS YIN AND YANG?

Diagnosing health problems in TCM is based on several different theories and concepts, one of them being the Yin Yang Theory. This theory is based on the idea that everything in the universe can be attributed to Yin and Yang: two opposing qualities that need each other in order to exist.

Yin represents the following characteristics: nighttime, darkness, cold, rest, moisture and softness. In contrast, Yang represents daytime, brightness, heat, activity, dryness and hardness. Nothing is ever all Yin or all Yang: everything is a balance of both qualities. Sometimes our bodies have too much Yang or too little Yin and any kind of imbalance may cause a health problem.

THE QI THEORY

The Qi Theory is based on the idea that everything in the universe is made up of **Qi** (say 'chee'), also known as vital energy or energy flow. There are specific pathways in our bodies called **meridians** where Qi flows. This Qi helps our **organs** function normally, but if the Qi in our bodies stop flowing smoothly, our bodies can experience health problems.

THE YIN YANG SYMBOL

The black part of the symbol represents Yin and the white part of the symbol represents Yang. Within Yin there is Yang and within Yang there is Yin.

6

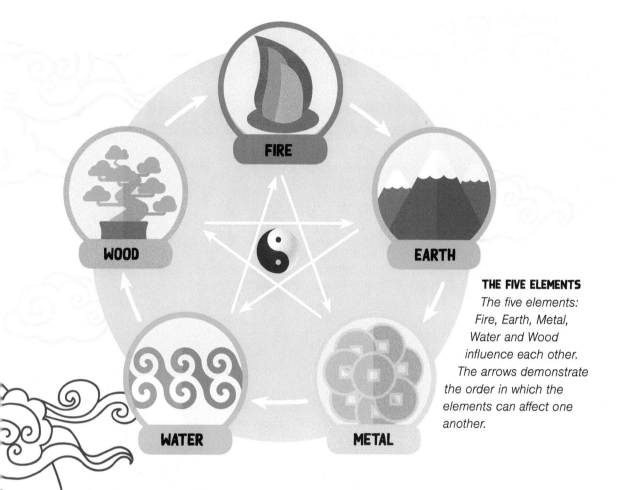

THE FIVE ELEMENTS
The five elements: Fire, Earth, Metal, Water and Wood influence each other. The arrows demonstrate the order in which the elements can affect one another.

THE FIVE ELEMENTS THEORY

The Five Elements Theory is based on the idea that five specific elements make up everything in the universe, including our bodies. This means that our bodies are a combination of Fire, Earth, Metal, Water and Wood. Each element represents specific body parts, colors, temperatures, emotions, tastes and more.

FIRE: heart, small **intestine**, **pericardium** (the sac that surrounds the heart), **triple energizer**, red, heat, joy, bitter, tongue.
EARTH: spleen, stomach, yellow, damp, thoughtful, sweet, mouth.

METAL: lung, large intestine, white, dry, sadness, strong-smelling, nose.
WATER: kidney, urinary bladder, black, cold, fear, salty, ears.
WOOD: liver, gall bladder, green, wind, anger, sour, eyes.

A TCM doctor can identify a health problem by carefully observing these signs on their patients. For example, if a patient gets 'angry' easily, this suggests that the wood element has been affected, more specifically the liver meridian (the organ related to the wood element). A constant 'bitter' taste in the mouth, suggests the fire element has been affected, more specifically the heart meridian (the organ related to the fire element).

WHY IT'S IMPORTANT TO CONTROL OUR EMOTIONS

TCM states that as long as everything inside and outside us is in harmony, our bodies can be healthy. All things, including our organs, Yin, Yang, Qi, and our environment, must be in balance.

But sometimes situations in our lives cause an imbalance in our bodies, making us sick.

Some of the main causes of disease are:
1. Climatic factors such as wind, summer heat, fire, dampness, dryness, and cold that can enter through the skin, mouth and nose
2. Emotional troubles
3. An unhealthy diet
4. Too much or too little exercise
5. Trauma or insect bites

Even our emotions should be felt in moderation as too much of anything can be harmful to our bodies. Too much anger affects the liver, too much joy can affect the heart, too much sadness affects the lungs, too much worry affects the spleen and too much fear affects the kidneys and the heart. Next time you are emotionally distressed, remind yourself to take deep breaths and try to calm down because it is better for your health.

IMPORTANT BODY SIGNS YOU MUST KNOW

In order to find out what illness a patient has, a TCM doctor has to ask specific questions about the patient's symptoms, make careful observations, take their **pulse**, (check the beating of their heart through the blood vessels in the wrist) and use their sense of smell and hearing, if necessary.

All of these things are done so that TCM doctors can better understand a patient's body condition. The goal is to find out whether a patient has more signs of Yin or Yang (such as cold or hot body signs), whether the sickness is located deep in the body, such as in the Qi, blood, or bone, or if it's located in a part of the body that isn't very deep, such as on the skin, hair, nails or meridians. They will try and find out whether a sickness is caused because there is too much of something, such as excess Yang, or too little of something, such as a Yang deficiency.

A TCM doctor may ask questions like: What do your **stools** (poop) look like? What is the color of your **urine**? You might think these questions are pretty disgusting, but our waste gives us important clues about our body's condition. Our stools and urine can change when we get sick – they don't always change, but sometimes they do and these are some of the signs that TCM doctors look for:

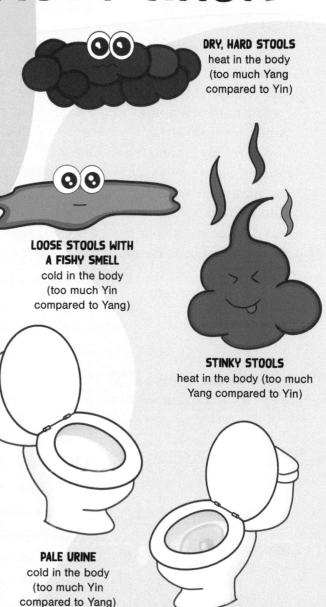

DRY, HARD STOOLS
heat in the body
(too much Yang compared to Yin)

LOOSE STOOLS WITH A FISHY SMELL
cold in the body
(too much Yin compared to Yang)

STINKY STOOLS
heat in the body (too much Yang compared to Yin)

PALE URINE
cold in the body
(too much Yin compared to Yang)

YELLOW-RED OR DARK URINE
heat in the body (too much Yang compared to Yin)

EIGHT DIFFERENT PULSES AND THEIR MEANINGS

When the body is sick, the pulse (heartbeat rate and quality) changes, therefore, TCM doctors take their patient's pulse to figure out what kind of health problem they may have. The pulse is taken by carefully feeling the patient's **radial artery** located on the wrist (below the thumb), by using the index finger, middle finger and ring finger. After lots of practice, a TCM doctor is able to feel the difference of over twenty pulses with different speeds, depths, and strengths.

In English:
Feel the pulse
In Chinese: 把脉 (Bǎ Mài)
Say: *Bah Mai*

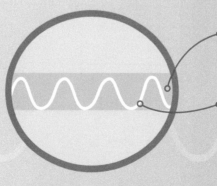

HOW TO TAKE A PULSE
A pulse is taken by using gentle pressure, followed by stronger pressure on 3 sections of the radial artery, in order to feel the depth and quality of the pulse.

NORMAL PULSE
A normal pulse should be calm and smooth, with 4 beats per breath (not too rapid and not too slow).

BASE LINE
There are 3 levels of depth: superficial, middle, and deep. The base line represents the middle level.

PULSE LINE
The pulse line represents the heartbeat rate and quality felt on the radial artery.

SUPERFICIAL PULSE can be felt with a light touch and represents a problem that is located in a part of the body that isn't very deep.

DEEP PULSE is felt near the bone and can represent a problem that is located deep inside the body.

SLOW PULSE has fewer than four beats per breath and represents cold.

TRY TAKING A FRIEND'S PULSE TO SEE WHAT KIND THEY HAVE.

TIGHT PULSE is a pulse that feels firm, forceful and vibrates – it represents cold or pain.

RAPID PULSE has more than four beats per breath and represents heat.

STRONG PULSE is a pulse that feels forceful and represents too much Qi and blood.

WEAK PULSE is a pulse that has no force and represents not having enough Qi and blood.

TONGUES SAY MORE THAN WORDS

In TCM our body parts are all connected, therefore our body's condition can be reflected in many different areas of the body, including our tongues. Observing a patient's tongue is an easy way for TCM doctors to check how the rest of their body is. By looking at the size, color, areas and quality of the tongue, a TCM doctor can identify a patient's imbalances.

PALE
Not enough Qi and blood

WHITE COATING
Too much cold

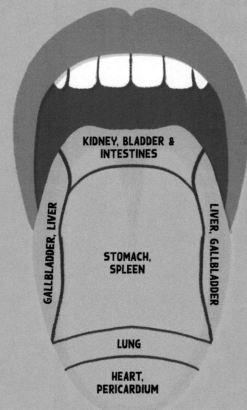

KIDNEY, BLADDER & INTESTINES

GALLBLADDER, LIVER

LIVER, GALLBLADDER

STOMACH, SPLEEN

LUNG

HEART, PERICARDIUM

TONGUE MAP
When one of these areas change color or texture, it suggests that the meridian of that organ is unbalanced.

YELLOW COATING
Too much heat

RED
Too much heat

PURPLE
Blood, cold or heat in
the body that isn't
moving smoothly

CRACKED TONGUE
Too much heat that is
harming body fluids, or
not enough blood

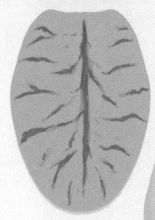

THIN COATING
A problem that is
located in a part of
the body that isn't
very deep

NORMAL
Healthy body
condition

TONGUE DIAGNOSIS

A healthy person should have a pink
tongue that is a little moist with a thin,
white coating. But when we get sick our
tongues change. Next time you get sick,
look in the mirror and see if your tongue
has changed in any of the following ways.

STICKY COATING
Damp, phlegm, or food
stuck in the body

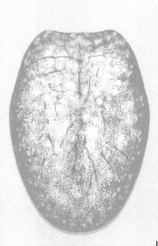

DRY COATING
Too much heat

EXCESSIVE MOISTURE
Upward flooding of harmful water
and cold, dampness

THICK COATING
Dampness,
phlegm, or food
stuck in the body

ACUPUNCTURE:
SPECIAL POINTS
ON OUR BODY

Acupuncture and acupressure are forms of treatments that have been used for thousands of years in China and other Asian countries, such as Korea and Japan. Only recently it has started to become popular in Western countries, such as the United States.

In English: Acupuncture
In Chinese: 针灸 (Zhēn Jiǔ)
Say: *Jen Jee-oh*

In English: Acupressure
In Chinese: 指压 (Zhǐ Yā)
Say: *Jir Ya*

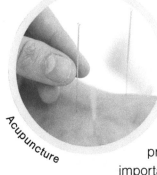
Acupuncture

ACUPUNCTURE is a method that uses thin needles to stimulate locations on the meridians, known as acupuncture points or **acupoints**, to treat health problems. It is extremely important to know the anatomy of the body in detail to correctly locate acupoints, therefore only licensed TCM doctors can perform acupuncture.

ACUPRESSURE, on the other hand, is a method used in Tuina massage to stimulate these points by using pressure, rather than using needles. This is an easy way for people to treat themselves. Acupressure can be done by applying firm pressure to acupoints using the index finger or thumb.

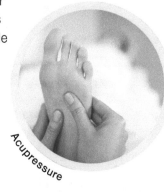
Acupressure

BUT HOW DOES ACUPUNCTURE WORK?

According to TCM, the meridians in our body correspond to different organs and have different functions. Once the doctor finds out what organ or meridian has a problem, the doctor can perform acupuncture on the sick meridians. The acupuncture needles don't have any magic healing powers, they are simply used to stimulate points on the meridians, which then allow the patient's own body to bring attention to those problem areas. The patient's own body does all the work, with just some help from the acupuncture needles. There are over 300 acupoints on the body with different functions to treat different illnesses.

When you get a cut on your finger, your own body brings attention to your finger to begin the healing process. So, acupuncture and acupressure aren't strange concepts as our bodies try to heal themselves all the time. But by intentionally stimulating specific areas on our body, we can tell it exactly which areas need attention.

SOME OF THE MOST COMMONLY USED ACUPOINTS:

HEART 7 (on the wrist crease below the pinky finger) Helps to relax the patient and treats **insomnia** and palpitations

PERICARDIUM 6 (about a three-finger width above the wrist crease, between the two tendons) Treats nausea and helps patients to relax

BAI CHONG WO (about a four-finger width above the border of the knee) Relieves itchiness

DU 20 (midpoint between two ears) Helps mental problems such as epilepsy, depression, insomnia and headaches

YIN TANG (midpoint between the eyebrows) Helps relax the patient and reduces pain

DU 26 (upper third between the nose and the lips) Wakes patient up from fainting and seizures (this is an emergency point)

REN 17 (midpoint between the nipples) Treats **asthma** and coughs

LARGE INTESTINE 11 (at the end of the elbow crease) Treats fever and abdominal pain

LUNG 7 (about a two-finger width above the wrist, on the side of the arm below the thumb) Treats coughs and sore throat

LARGE INTESTINE 4 (the sensitive area between the index finger and the thumb) Helps relax the patient and reduces pain, such as a headache and sore throat

STOMACH 36 (about a four-finger width below the knee and one-finger width to the side of the shin) Helps digestion, diarrhea, and constipation

KIDNEY 3 (between the bone and the tendon found on the inner side of the foot) Treats insomnia, dizziness, sore throat, toothache, asthma and irregular periods

EAR ACUPUNCTURE

Our ears also have lots of useful acupoints that represent different parts of our bodies. Both acupuncture and acupressure can be performed on the ear to treat problems related to those body parts.

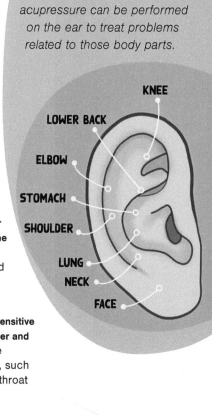

KNEE
LOWER BACK
ELBOW
STOMACH
SHOULDER
LUNG
NECK
FACE

ACUPUNCTURE NEEDLES

Can you believe in ancient times, acupuncture was performed with a stone needle? Nowadays, acupuncture is less scary, and some patients say they don't even feel the needles. Acupuncture needles are thinner than injection needles, they are as thin as a strand of hair.

WHAT IS CUPPING?

Have you ever seen athletes with circular bruises on their backs? These bruises are from cupping, a method that uses suction cups to stimulate the meridians on different parts of the body, commonly done on the back for about fifteen minutes.

This is not only relaxing, but it also helps with pain, inflammation, blood flow, and the regular function of the cupped acupoint. After cupping, a TCM doctor can even observe the color of the bruises to know more detail about the patient's problem.

BRUISING SIGNS

A PALE COLOR
means there isn't enough blood or Qi in that area.

A PURPLE BRUISE
means there's stagnation, in other words, blood or Qi isn't moving smoothly.

A PINKISH BRUISE
means there's a healthy blood flow.

HERBAL MEDICINE:
TEAS AND DECOCTIONS

In English: Tea
In Chinese: 茶 (Chá)
Say: Cha

Medicinal herbs used by TCM doctors include roots, bark, twigs, leaves, flowers, seeds and fruits. Sometimes they may even use animal products. There are hundreds of commonly used herbs that are used to make decoctions and teas.

Decoctions are strong medicinal recipes that TCM doctors prescribe to their patients, containing around six or more herbs, boiled for at least thirty minutes. Each herb has a different function and the functions can change when mixed with other herbs. Teas, on the other hand, are made by simply soaking herbs in boiling water for a few minutes. Teas are not as strong as decoctions; therefore, they are more commonly used. Both decoctions and teas can be useful, but they don't usually work right away – they usually take a few weeks of drinking to have an effect on your body.

MORE THAN **100** COMMONLY USED WESTERN MEDICINE DRUGS ARE MADE FROM HERBS, SUCH AS ALOE, ASPIRIN, AND PENICILLIN. USING HERBS FOR TREATMENT ISN'T A NEW OR STRANGE IDEA: HERBS ARE VERY USEFUL IN THE WORLD OF MEDICINE.

HOW CAN I EAT HEALTHY FOOD?

Food is one of the most important factors for a body to stay healthy. Just because somebody hasn't experienced a serious illness yet, it doesn't mean they won't in the future.

People who grow up eating unhealthy food, usually get lots of illnesses as they grow older so it is very important to eat healthily from a young age. Food can affect your appearance and how you feel emotionally and physically. The key to a healthy diet is to eat a lot of different unprocessed foods, like different-colored fruits and vegetables.

CARROTS
According to TCM, they strengthen Qi, clear excessive heat and remove **toxins**. According to Western medicine, carrots help lower **cholesterol**, prevent **cataracts** and **night blindness**.

SWEET POTATOES
According to TCM, they strengthen Qi, help the spleen and stomach and balance Qi and blood. According to Western medicine, they help prevent **constipation** and keep the **immune system** healthy.

BROCCOLI
According to TCM, this improves Qi circulation and cools heat in the body. According to Western medicine, broccoli helps fight elements that may cause cancer.

SPINACH
According to TCM, this nourishes the blood, Yin and clears heat. According to Western medicine, it can help prevent fractures by keeping the bones strong and it keeps **blood pressure** low.

YIN FOODS VS. YANG FOODS

If a patient has more Yin in their body, they should eat less Yin food and more Yang food, in order to balance their body. If a patient has more Yang in their body, they should eat less Yang food and more Yin food. Yang food can warm your body and Yin food can cool your body.

YIN FOODS
banana, apple, watermelon, orange, strawberry, lemon, cucumber, carrot, lettuce, celery, spinach, tofu, crab, green tea, peppermint tea, chrysanthemum tea, and cold drinks.

YANG FOODS
cherry, mango, peach, raspberry, red dates, onion, pumpkin, ginger, cinnamon, chestnut, walnut, beef, pork, chicken, ginseng, jasmine tea, rosemary, most sweets, coffee and alcohol (for adults).

A COLORFUL MEAL
The more colorful your plate is, the more nutritious your meal will be.

19

DR. VALENTINA
OPENS THE TCM CLINIC

Dr. Valentina is a TCM doctor. She starts her day off by putting her white coat on and welcomes her first patient, James, into her office.

In English:
Chrysanthemum Flower Tea
In Chinese: 菊花茶(Júhuā Chá)
Say: Joo-hwa Cha

CASE 1

Recently, James decided to play outside without wearing a cozy jacket, so he has a cold now. He feels chills and has a fever.

Dr. Valentina asks to see his tongue. She notices that he has a thin, white coating on it.

THIN WHITE COATING
Too much cold

Then, Valentina asks James to sit down so she can feel his pulse while he is feeling calm. His pulse is superficial and tight.

James is showing signs of 'wind cold'.

SUPERFICIAL AND TIGHT PULSE:
a pulse that feels firm, forceful and vibrates, felt with a light touch – it represents cold or pain located in a part of the body that isn't very deep.

DR. VALENTINA PRESCRIBES
'Ginger and Brown Sugar Tea'. Ginger and Brown Sugar Tea is used to treat the common cold, specifically for someone who feels cold and isn't sweating. This tea is also used to balance the stomach, for problems like stomach pain, nausea, and vomiting.

GINGER AND BROWN SUGAR TEA
3-5 slices of uncooked ginger and brown sugar

Dr. Valentina also recommends James to eat Yang foods, such as ginseng chicken soup with red dates, to warm up his body. Dr. Valentina then performs acupuncture on Lung 7, and Large Intestine 4.

CASE 2

While James is fast asleep in one room during his acupuncture treatment, Dr. Valentina's second patient, Ralph, arrives. Ralph has also got a cold but he has different symptoms.

He has a fever, but unlike James, he is sweating and his tongue has a yellowish coating.

THIN YELLOW COATING
Too much heat

His pulse is superficial and rapid. Dr. Valentina gives Ralph a different treatment because even though James and Ralph both have a cold, they have different body conditions and different symptoms, meaning that they need different treatments.

Ralph is showing signs of 'wind heat'.

SUPERFICIAL AND RAPID PULSE:
has more than four beats per breath and can be felt with a light touch - it represents heat located in a part of the body that isn't very deep.

DR. VALENTINA PRESCRIBES

'Chrysanthemum Flower Tea'. Chrysanthemum Flower Tea is used to treat the common cold, specifically for someone showing heat signs. This tea is also used to lower high blood pressure, and to treat headaches and dizziness.

CHRYSANTHEMUM FLOWER TEA

4-5 Chrysanthemum flowers

Dr. Valentina also recommends Ralph to eat more Yin foods, such as a smoothie made with celery, apples, and carrots, to cool his body down. Dr. Valentina then performs acupuncture on Large Intestine 11, and Large Intestine 4.

HOW TO MAKE TEA

1. With adult supervision, heat water in an electric kettle or by placing a kettle on the stove.
2. Pour hot water into a cup.
3. Steep tea for about 4 minutes.
4. Remove tea and enjoy.

In English: Rush Pith
In Chinese: 灯芯草
(Dēngxīn Cǎo)
Say: *Dung-sheen Tsa-oh*

Dr. Valentina welcomes in her third patient, Aurora. Aurora loves to sleep, but she's been feeling pretty grouchy lately because she's been having trouble falling asleep. She has insomnia.

Dr. Valentina takes a look at Aurora's tongue and sees that her tongue is red.

RED
Too much heat

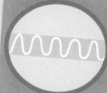

She then feels her pulse, which is rapid. She asks Aurora a little bit more about her symptoms.

RAPID PULSE
has more than four beats per breath and represents heat.

Dr. Valentina asks Aurora what color and quality her stools are, what color her urine is, and whether she feels hot or cold usually.

Aurora says her stools are dry and hard, her urine is dark yellow, and she usually feels hot.

DRY, HARD STOOLS: heat in the body (too much Yang compared to Yin)

YELLOW-RED OR DARK URINE: heat in the body (too much Yang compared to Yin)

DR. VALENTINA PRESCRIBES

a sleeping tea. From all of those signs, Dr. Valentina can tell she has heat in her body, so she prescribes a sleeping tea that treats insomnia (a problem falling asleep or staying asleep) for people with heat signs in their body.

SLEEPING TEA
10-20 grams of Rush Pith

Dr. Valentina also recommends Aurora to eat less Yang food, such as sweets and coffee, which may be causing her to have insomnia. Dr. Valentina then does acupuncture on Heart 7, Kidney 3, Pericardium 6, DU 20, and Yin Tang.

ACUPUNCTURE POINTS
See page 15

CASE 4

It's a pretty busy day in the clinic. The next patient, Sofia, walks into the clinic complaining about an itchy insect bite.

DR. VALENTINA PRESCRIBES

'tea leaves'. She knows that they are the perfect thing to relieve itchiness. Tea leaves are used to stop pain, itching and swelling due to bee stings or other insect bites.

TEA LEAVES

Tea leaves or a tea bag soaked in boiling water and then once cooled off, applied on top of the skin.

Dr. Valentina then performs acupuncture on the Bai Chong Wo acupoint.

ACUPUNCTURE POINTS
See page 15

CASE 5

The next patient, Marcel, suffers from asthma and his tongue has a white coating. His pulse is superficial and tight. Dr. Valentina diagnoses him with 'wind cold' causing asthma.

DR. VALENTINA PRESCRIBES

'Tangerine Peel Tea'. Tangerine Peel Tea can be used to treat coughs, asthma, to strengthen the stomach, and even make skin beautiful.

TANGERINE PEEL TEA

Fresh tangerine peel and white sugar (optional)

ACUPUNCTURE POINTS
See page 15

Dr. Valentina recommends Marcel to eat less dairy food, which can cause an excess of phlegm in the body and worsen asthma. Lastly, Dr. Valentina does acupuncture on Lung 7 and Large Intestine 4.

In English: Tangerine Peel tea
In Chinese: 陈皮茶 (Chénpí Chá)
Say: *Chen-pee Cha*

23

GAME TIME:
SEE IF YOU CAN HELP THE DOCTOR?

See if you can help the doctor by diagnosing his patients. Choose the correct multiple-choice answer according to the patient's body signs.

QUIZ 1

Alex comes to the clinic because he's been feeling nauseous recently. His tongue has a thick, white coating and his pulse is deep and slow.

What do you think is Alex's problem?
A) Wind Heat
B) Not enough Qi
C) Cold in the Stomach

Which tea do you think would be best for Alex's problem?
A) Fresh Tangerine Peel Tea
B) Ginger and Brown Sugar Tea
C) Chrysanthemum Flower Tea

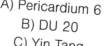

What food should Alex eat?
A) Cold Banana Smoothie
B) Lettuce, Cucumber, and Carrot salad
C) Chicken Pumpkin Soup

Which acupressure point would be useful for Alex's problem?
A) Pericardium 6
B) DU 20
C) Yin Tang

DEEP AND
SLOW PULSE

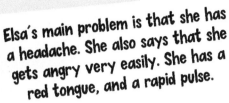

QUIZ 2

Elsa's main problem is that she has a headache. She also says that she gets angry very easily. She has a red tongue, and a rapid pulse.

What do you think is Elsa's problem?
(Hint: Which organ represents anger?)
- A) Cold in the Spleen
- B) Lung Heat
- C) Excess Liver Yang

Which tea do you think would be best for Elsa's problem?
- A) Chrysanthemum Flower Tea
- B) Ginger and Brown Sugar Tea
- C) Fresh Tangerine Peel Tea

What food should Elsa eat?
- A) Ginseng Chicken Soup with Red Dates
- B) Carrot Salad
- C) Cinnamon Latte

Which acupressure point would be useful for Elsa's problem?
- A) Large Intestine 4
- B) Ren 17
- C) Bai Chong Wo

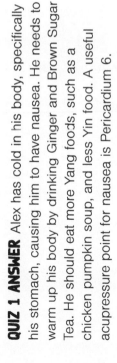

QUIZ 2 ANSWER

Elsa has an excess of Liver Yang in her body which is causing her to have headaches and to feel very angry. She needs to cool her body down by drinking Chrysanthemum Flower Tea, and she should eat more Yin foods, such as a carrot salad. A useful acupressure point for headaches is Large Intestine 4.

QUIZ 1 ANSWER Alex has cold in his body, specifically his stomach, causing him to have nausea. He needs to warm up his body by drinking Ginger and Brown Sugar Tea. He should eat more Yang foods, such as a chicken pumpkin soup, and less Yin food. A useful acupressure point for nausea is Pericardium 6.

PUZZLES AND GAMES

1

WHICH TREATMENT IS THIS?
_____
A: CUPPING
B: ACUPUNCTURE
C: ACUPRESSURE

2

GUESS WHICH FOODS ARE YIN AND WHICH ARE YANG?

mango
lemon
peach
strawberry
watermelon
orange
banana
cherry
raspberry

3

? WHICH SIDE IS YANG?

? WHICH SIDE IS YIN?

---

1. WHICH TREATMENT?
A: Cupping
See pages 14-15 for more information.

2. FOODS
Yin foods: banana, strawberry, lemon, orange, watermelon. Yang foods: mango, cherry, raspberry, peach.
See page 17 for more information.

4 LET'S MATCH THE RIGHT WORDS TO THE ELEMENTS

WOOD

FIRE

EARTH

METAL

WATER

WHICH COLOR BELONGS TO EACH ELEMENT?	WHICH BODY PART BELONGS TO EACH ELEMENT?	WHICH CLIMATE BELONGS TO EACH ELEMENT?	WHICH EMOTION BELONGS TO EACH ELEMENT?
BLACK	LIVER	DRY	JOY
RED	SPLEEN	HEAT	FEAR
YELLOW	KIDNEY	COLD	SADNESS
GREEN	HEART	DAMP	THOUGHTFUL
WHITE	LUNG	WINDY	ANGER

5 WHICH POO? MATCH THE POOP TO WHAT IT MEANS

LOOSE STOOLS WITH A FISHY SMELL

A: HEAT IN THE BODY (TOO MUCH YANG COMPARED TO YIN)

B: COLD IN THE BODY (TOO MUCH YIN COMPARED TO YANG)

DRY, HARD STOOLS

---

3. WHICH SIDE IS YIN? WHICH SIDE IS YANG?
The black part of the symbol represents Yin and the white part represents Yang.
See page 6 for more information.

4. ELEMENTS MATCHING GAME
Fire: red, heart, heat, joy. **Earth:** yellow, spleen, damp, thoughtful. **Metal:** white, lung, dry, sadness. **Water:** black, kidney, cold, fear. **Wood:** green, liver, wind, anger.
See page 7 for more information.

5. POOP
Dry, hard stools means there's heat in the body. Loose stools with a fishy smell means there's cold in the body.
See page 9 for more information.

HOW TO BECOME A TCM DOCTOR

In ancient times, TCM knowledge was passed down in the family. Nowadays, it's not necessary to have a parent or grandparent to pass down the knowledge about the hundreds of acupuncture points and herbs with different functions.

In English: Doctor
In Chinese: 医生 (Yīshēng)
Say: *Ee-shohng*

This book was intended to give you a simple introduction to natural medicine and to inspire you to follow your dreams. I encourage you to read more advanced TCM books, as well as to practice your skills of differentiating tongues and pulses. Look at your friends' tongues and compare them to your own; how are they different? This isn't an easy task – it takes years to master. Once you are ready to attend a college or a university, you can major in TCM (3-5 years) and become a TCM doctor.

I WISH YOU THE BEST OF LUCK!

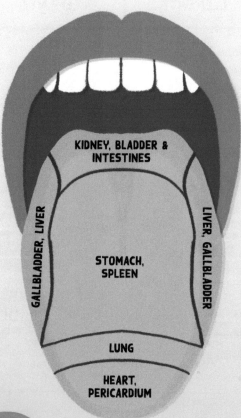

KIDNEY, BLADDER & INTESTINES

GALLBLADDER, LIVER

LIVER, GALLBLADDER

STOMACH, SPLEEN

LUNG

HEART, PERICARDIUM

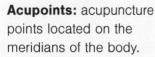

GLOSSARY

Acupoints: acupuncture points located on the meridians of the body.

Acupressure: a method that uses pressure instead of needles to stimulate acupoints.

Acupuncture: a treatment method that uses thin needles to stimulate meridian points on the body.

Asthma: a condition in which people experience difficulty breathing with wheezing, coughing, and tightness in the chest.

Blood pressure: the pressure of the blood on the walls of blood vessels, which can change depending on various things, such as age, diet, and stress.

Cataract: an eye problem in which the lens of the eye is cloudy.

Cholesterol: an important waxy substance that is seen in animal cells and tissues, that can also harden and thicken the blood vessels if there is too much of this substance.

Constipation: a condition marked by difficult or irregular bowel movements.

Cupping: a method that uses suction cups to stimulate the meridians or acupoints.

Decoction: strong medicinal recipes that TCM doctors prescribe to their patients, containing around six or more herbs, boiled for at least thirty minutes.

Five Elements Theory: a theory that is based on the idea that five specific elements (Fire, Earth, Metal, Water, and Wood) make up everything in the universe, including our bodies.

Food therapy: the use of healthy food to balance the body and stay healthy.

Immune system: a system that helps protect the body from harmful substances.

Insomnia: a condition marked by not being able to fall asleep or stay asleep.

Intestines: a long tube that connects the stomach to the anus, that helps digest food, absorb nutrients, and eliminates waste.

Meridians: specific pathways or channels of energy, known as Qi, that flow within our bodies.

Natural medicine: a form of healthcare that avoids drugs and surgery, and uses physical exercise, physical manipulations, diet and natural substances such as herbs for prevention and treatment.

Night Blindness: a condition marked by normal vision in daylight and poor vision at night or in dim light.

Organs: a grouping of tissues that perform a specific task, e.g. lungs, heart, liver.

Pericardium: the sac that surrounds the heart.

Phlegm: a slippery, sticky, thick substance made in the body, that is usually eliminated through the mouth.

Pulse: the beating of the heart, that can be felt through the blood vessels.

Qi: the vital energy or energy flow that creates everything in the universe.

Qigong: an exercise that combines breathing, movements and meditation in order to improve one's health.

Radial artery: a blood vessel, felt on the underside of the forearm, beneath the base of the thumb.

Stools: waste that is eliminated through the anus, also known as poop.

Theory of Qi: a theory that is based on the idea that everything in the universe is made up of Qi.

Toxins: substances that create disharmony within the body, such as harmful or poisonous substances.

Triple Energizer: the areas of the body where food, water, and fluid pass through. It is made up of three sections of the trunk of the body, (the trunk is the part without the head, arms and legs). The three sections of the Triple Energizer are: the upper trunk between the neck and the lower ribs, including the heart and lungs; the middle trunk from the lower ribs to the navel, including the stomach and spleen; the lower trunk from the navel to the tops of the legs, including the bladder and the intestines.

Traditional Chinese Medicine: a form of medicine that uses several theories, such as the Yin Yang Theory, the Theory of Qi, and the Five Elements

Theory to identify a problem. It then uses acupuncture, herbal medicine, Tuina, cupping, food therapy, and Qigong as a treatment.

Tuina: a medical massage that stimulates acupoints.

Urine: a liquid waste discharged by the kidneys, also known as pee.

Western medicine: a form of medicine that uses scientific evidence to identify a problem and then uses surgery or drugs as a treatment.

Yin Yang Theory: a theory based on the idea that everything in the universe can be attributed to Yin and Yang: two opposing qualities that need each other in order to exist.

Yin and Yang: two opposing qualities that need each other in order to exist.

ACKNOWLEDGEMENTS

I would like to thank the following:
My mother, Acupuncture Physician and Physical Therapist, Franse Lozada; she inspired me to pursue an amazing career in the medical field just as she did. The creation of this book wouldn't have been possible without her.

My father, brothers, husband, family and friends (Valentina Taborda and Elsa Lee), who have all inspired me to write this book and have helped me throughout the process.

INDEX

CPSIA information can be obtained
at www.ICGtesting.com
Printed in the USA
BVHW091545141221
624016BV00002B/61

* 9 7 8 1 7 3 5 0 5 7 5 0 7 *